Powershell

The ultimate beginner's guide to Powershell, making you a master at Windows Powershell command line fast!

Table of Contents

Introduction 1

Chapter 1: Learning About the PowerShell Language 2

Chapter 2: Working with the Commands in PowerShell 5

Chapter 3: Pipelines and Outputs on PowerShell 10

Chapter 4: The Operations and Wildcards of PowerShell 18

Chapter 5: Doing Quotes and Strings in PowerShell 25

Chapter 6: Scalers and What They Mean in PowerShell...........31

Chapter 7: The Drives and Providers 38

Conclusion.. 43

Introduction

Thank you for taking the time to pick up this book about PowerShell!

This book covers the topic of Windows PowerShell and will teach you all about how to use it and all of its possibilities. Basically, the PowerShell is a command line interface that operates within the Windows system, with the purpose of task automation and configuration management. It is a fairly intuitive system, and as you will soon realize, doesn't take too long to get the hang of.

In the following chapters, you will learn how the PowerShell operates, how the associated scripting language works, the different commands you will need to know, and what kind of things are possible when using the PowerShell.

Even if you're totally new to programming and have never used a scripting environment, at the completion of this book you should have a solid understanding of Windows PowerShell, and be ready to get started!

Once again, thanks for choosing this book, I hope you find it to be helpful!

Chapter 1: Learning About the PowerShell Language

When it comes to the world of coding, there are a lot of different languages that you are able to use. To those who have never done any coding, the idea of these languages can seem confusing, but it is similar to learning Greek, Italian, Spanish, or German when your native language is English. You will need to learn some of the basic words, what they mean to your own language, and how to form sentences (or commands) in order to get them to work the way that you would like. This can take some time to learn, and just like vocal languages, some coding languages are easier, and others will take a bit more time to understand.

There are many different types of coding languages that you can choose from, each with their own uses and capabilities. Some people like to work with Python because it has a decent amount of power while still being easy enough for a beginner to learn. For those who would like to learn how to create websites and add-ons for websites, Java and JavaScript are the best languages to go with. C and C++ are good ones to learn when you want a lot of power behind your coding language. All of these have their uses depending on what you are trying to achieve.

In this guidebook, we are going to spend some time talking about PowerShell from Microsoft. This is basically a new Command Line Interface that is used for the Windows system. If you like how Windows works and are pretty familiar with the system, this can be a good choice for enhancing your Windows experience. It is a good one to use because it uses the simple Microsoft interface but it also has a lot of power. Let's take a look at how the PowerShell language works and why you should consider using it for your coding needs.

What is the PowerShell?

PowerShell is a shell that has been developed by Microsoft to help with configuration management and task automation. This is a powerful shell that is based on the .NET framework. It comes with a command line shell and its own scripting language for you to employ.

In addition to the command line shell that comes with this, you are also going to find the Windows PowerShell ISE. This stands for Integrated Scripting Environment, and is essentially a user interface that is graphical and allows you to create a lot of different scripts without having to type all of your commands into the command line each time.

So basically, the PowerShell is a command line interface that you are able to use with the Windows system. It comes ready with everything you need to begin, including:

- Access to the Dynamic Linked Libraries with Windows

- Access to the Windows COM

- Access to Windows Management Instrumentation

- Access to the .Net Framework API

- PowerShell Functions

- PowerShell Commands

- Existing Windows Command Line Tools

As you can see, there are a lot of features that come with PowerShell, and you will also be able to get access to many other APIs and technologies that are already available on the Windows system. This is one of the things that makes the PowerShell so popular.

Another added benefit is that the PowerShell is already included with your Windows System. If you have Windows 2008 or Windows 7, you are going to have the PowerShell v2 version, while the PowerShell v3 is going to be found on Windows 2012 and Windows 8. If you don't have these systems in place, you can also download the PowerShell here: http://support.microsoft.com/kb/968929.

What can I do with PowerShell?

At this point, you are probably wondering what exactly you can achieve with this great scripting language.

The PowerShell was originally designed as a tool to help the user automate and solve a lot of the tedious admin tasks that exist on your computer. For example, you can use this coding language in order to display all of the USB devices that are installed on either one or more of the computers that are on your network. You can use this coding language to identify and also kill processes that are not responding properly, and even to filter out some specific information about a computer that is on your network.

The Powershell helps to simplify as well as automate some of the repetitive, and sometimes tedious, tasks that you need to do as the admin. It can create scripts for these tasks and will also combine a few different commands together to make things easier.

Many network administrators find that the PowerShell is helpful to them when it comes to working in the Active Directory. Due to the fact that the PowerShell contains hundreds of commands that you can customize (these commands are called 'cmdlets'), the degree of help that the PowerShell will provide you in becoming more productive and efficient in your network is pretty high.

Essentially, the PowerShell is going to make it easier to run your network as the admin without having to waste time and energy working on tedious tasks. It is a simple and clear system that has the ability to take over a lot of boring processes, allowing you to keep everything on the Windows system organized in an efficient way.

Chapter 2: Working with the Commands in PowerShell

One thing that you will notice when using PowerShell is that it has its own language for coding. While some of the other shells available allow you to use Python, C#, C++ or one of the other coding languages, this one relies on its own language to complete its processes. This may seem like a bit of a pain for those who may already know a coding language and don't want to learn a whole new one to use this system, but PowerShell does keep things simple. Whether you know other coding languages or not, you will find that the commands in PowerShell are pretty easy to learn and get the hang of.

When we are talking about coding languages, the 'command' is the part that is going to make a specific action occur. The command could be in charge of retrieving contents from a folder, or updating an entry into your registry. So basically the 'command' is going to be compared to how the 'function' will work in many other coding languages. PowerShell has over 100 commands that are built in, and you are also able to create some of your own commands if needed.

The naming protocol of commands in PowerShell is that you will write them in the verb-noun form. This helps to keep things consistent, and can also help you to learn faster. The verb is going to be the action part of your command and then the noun is going to tell the command where the action should be performed. In order to get a command to run on this system, you will need to bring up the command prompt, similar to what you would see with Linux or some of the other operating systems, type in the requirements using the syntax that we gave above, and then hit Enter. If you did the process correctly, you should see the right outcome occur.

At times, you may forget some of the commands that you want to use inside of PowerShell. This is going to happen often in the beginning when you are first learning how to use Powershell. There is no need to fret or spend hours looking online to find the

5

command that you want. The Get-Command is going to help you out here.

When you use the Get-Command, you will tell the system to provide you with a full list of all the commands that it has available. This will provide you with a list of all the commands that are useful in PowerShell, and you will be able to simply choose the one that you want.

How does the command help work?

Inside of the PowerShell, you will notice that there is a sequence of Help files that you are able to use whenever you need them. You can access them by opening up the command window and then using the command "Get-Help". The system will then bring up all the other commands that you may need, as well as a description of how they all work.

When you make a command, there is going to be a hyphen in between the verb and the noun to separate them out, and to tell the command prompt what you would like to do.

Let's take a look at how this works with a few of the common tasks that an administrator may need to work on with text files. For example, if you would like to read through a file that has been sent through this system, you could use the command "Get-Content". If this is the only text file that is on the system, it is going to show up after you place this command into your command prompt and push enter.

Of course, there are often more than one text file on the computer at a time, and if you just put in the command like this, the computer system is not going to have any idea what you are actually looking for. You will simply need to put in a few more details in order to get this to work. Make sure that you know the name of the text file that you want to use, and then bring up the command prompt before typing "Get-Help 'name' Get-Content". This is going to return the command description and the syntax information. Keep in mind that the Get-Content command is also used to return the contents of an item, or to return any type of file on the system to the right place.

Using this command, you can have it bring up a text document that you want to read or bring up other files on the system, based on the syntax and the names that you put into the code.

Concepts Help

Any time that you are looking to get an overview of the different types of concepts that are inside of PowerShell, you will be able to use the Help files to find the information that you want. Each of these files is going to begin with "about_" and then it will end with the name of the topic. For example, you will be able to look at the complete list of these going alphabetically by entering the command: Get-Help about*

The example above is going to list out all the concepts that are on the computer, but this can get kind of long and boring, especially if you already know the name of the file that you want to use. You will just need to add in that name as a parameter value in the syntax and it will take you right there without having to go through all the other steps. For example, if you want to get a file that is concerned with flow control, you would simply need to enter the command "Get-Help about_flow_control" and then the command prompt will be able to handle the rest.

Aliases

There are a few commands in PowerShell that can be kind of wordy. While typing them out a few times may not seem like a big deal, if you have to type them very often however, it can get annoying and wastes a lot of time. Luckily, the PowerShell system allows you to use some aliases in order to refer to the various commands that you want. These are basically alternate names that you can use for your commands that will take up less space and time than the original - basically like a shortcut.

You will have the choice of either writing down the commands that you want to shorthand or you can use "Get-Alias" any time you want to see a list of all the aliases that you are able to use within the system.

Now, for a bit of clarification, it is important to note that the 'current session' refers to the current connection with PowerShell. When you first open up PowerShell, you are going to be creating a brand new session. This session is going to remain in effect until you close and exit out of PowerShell, which will effectively end the connection as well as the session. One thing that you are able to do during your sessions on PowerShell is look under Get-Alias and see what other aliases were created by users during that session, as well as any aliases that are defined in the startup, user configurations, or profiles.

If you would like to view a specified command' alias, you will then need to identify the specific Get-Alias command. For example, if you would like to view the aliases that you can use with Get-ChildItem, you will need to enter the following command:

Get-Alias |

Where-Object {$_.definition

-match "Get-ChildItem"}

At this point, there are probably a few parts of the command that you don't understand, but don't worry, we will go over those parts later on. However, it is important to learn that the outcome of this command is going to be directed to the Where-Object command so that you are able to filter out some of the results that may not match up with Get-ChildItem. You are able to do this with all the commands and aliases that you want, and you will simply need to change the name of the command to correspond with what you are looking for.

It is also important to note that PowerShell is going to utilize three different aliases that refer to Get-ChildItem and these will include dir, ls, and gci. Each of these are going to produce the same result. So basically, the three codes that are written below are all going to work the same in PowerShell:

Get-ChildItem c:/windows

dir c:/windows

ls c:/windows

gci c:/windows

If you are feeling a bit adventurous, you are able to create one of your own aliases inside the current session by using the command "Set-Alias". It is pretty easy to do. So let's say that you want to create an alias for Get-Content and you want to name it cnt; all you would need to do is run the command "Set-Alias cnt Get-Content".

Now you have basically created a brand new alias, and you will be able to use the shortcut 'cnt' any time that you would normally use Get-Content in the system. This alias is going to stay active until you end the PowerShell session.

Chapter 3: Pipelines and Outputs on PowerShell

So far in this guidebook we have learned that commands are one of the basics of working on this kind of program. These commands are going to make it easier to work inside of PowerShell because they will tell the system what we want to do. You can look up which programs you would like to open up and run, you can give them aliases, and so much more. But there is really quite a lot more that you will be able to do with the system outside of using the basic commands that we have discussed so far in this book.

While commands in PowerShell are pretty powerful and you are going to be able to do a lot with them, it may not always be enough to provide some of the outcomes that you want. Because the commands don't always have all the power that you need on their own, PowerShell has created pipelines to make things easier. These link commands together so that they are able to accomplish so much more, with much more complex tasks, compared to what the commands are able to do on their own. In this chapter, we are going to take some time to learn how to place commands into a pipeline with PowerShell in order to create illustrations, while also learning how to sort and then format the output of these illustrations within the system.

Working on the Pipelines

As we stated before, PowerShell is basically a system that is based off sets of commands which will pass on objects starting with one command and moving them on to the next. Each of these commands is going to create an object before sending it down the line, where the next command is going to pick it up. The command that picks up these objects will utilize the object as the input in order to create a brand new output before sending it on down to another command. This process is going to continue on until it reaches the conclusion that you want.

This chain of commands can be short or long and will create a pipeline that is held together with the help of the (|) symbol.

In a traditional command shell, the results from this pipeline are all going to be returned at once. This means that the results from the whole pipeline are going to be shown as just one result, and you won't see all the different steps in the pipeline. But with PowerShell, things are gong to work slightly differently. The results are going to be sent across this pipeline and once one of the commands has a result, it is going to be instantly accessible to the following command inside that pipeline.

For example, if you are using the Get-Service command, you will then get a rundown of each service that is currently in your framework. When this is done, you are going to see that the command is also going to give back the status, display, and name of all the administration on the system.

To go further, instead of seeing the entire rundown of services on the system, you choose to get a return of the list of services that are currently running on the system. To do this, you would need to use both the Get-Service and the Where-Object commands. You would need to write out these commands like the following in order to create your pipeline:

Get_Service | Where_Object {$_.status-eq 'running'}

As you can see, the pipeline operator is in place to show that the two commands are going to be connected. The Get-Service part of this is going to produce an object that will contain a full list of information that is service related. By using this symbol, the object is then going to be sent over to the Where-Object command as the input. The Where-Object command will then be used to filter the information based on what you placed inside the brackets so that you are able to just get the information that you need from this.

Now if it is found that the information inside of the braces is true, the object is then going to be sent along the pipeline, with the right filters in place, so that the information or objects that don't meet the criteria that you set out will be filtered from the results and you just get the information that you need.

With this example, we used the operator -eq, which means that the status property needs to be equal to the running string. Keep in mind that you will also be able to see all of the properties that are available with the Help files while the Status is a part that will generate an object with the help of the Get-service command. By passing along one or more objects in this pipeline, you are going to be able to access the properties just like you did earlier with the Where-Object.

Now say that you want to limit the information that is returned even more. Sometimes the information that is going to come back to you can be pretty large and if you are just looking for something in particular with your code, it can be challenging to go through and have to look through all the objects that will be returned from the previous commands. It is possible to get any of the information that you want returned as long as you send the right commands, and use the right pipeline, through the system to bring back the right results. In the following example, we are going to tell the system that we just want to display the name information in our returns:

Get-Service |

where {$_.status -eq 'running} |

select displayname

For the syntax above, the object is going to be received by the Select-Object command from the Where-Object command. This illustration is going to utilize the where alias in order to make reference to the Where-Object and then the select alias in order to go back and reference the Select-Object command. For select, you will be able to specify the property name that you want to display, which you will be able to specify with the displayname part (you can put in the name of any of the objects or processes that you would like to show up in this part). Once the information has been returned, you will be able to see that the data is already filtered based on your specifications.

When you are employing these pipelines, it is important that you remember that you are working on the process of operating with objects. Each of the commands that you are making will create an object that will then be received by the next. The final command that you have there is the one that will generate the object, which will then output the illustration results. Now we are going to move on to learning how to use these objects and their properties in order to refine the illustrations in PowerShell.

Working with the Format Output

One thing to note before we get into this section is that PowerShell is defaulted to automatically format illustrations based on the data type that is in the output. For example, if you use the Get-Process PS, you will get an illustration that can be used to return the data that is on the PS process. this is going to display the output of the command, and if you wish to have something else come up, you will just need to use the pipeline, along with one of the four supported format output commands that are supported with PowerShell to make it happen. The four commands that can help with this are:

- Format-Table – this is the command that is going to display the returned data inside the table, which is going to be the default of many of the commands. Because of this, it is not often that you will need to specify the output.

- Format-List – this command is going to return the data in a list form for you to look through.

- Format-Wide – this command is going to return the data through a wide table format. This table is going to include just one value for each of the items that are displayed.

- Format-Custom – with this command, you will be given data in the custom format, which is going to be based upon the configuration data that is saved on your computer. You will notice that it will come back in the .ps1xml file format and any time that you want to update it, you will just need to use Update-Format-Data.

Control the Output

Unless you go through and override it, the default output is going to be applied to the format before it is sent out to the output console window whenever the illustration has been executed. You can go through and override this by using one of the four commands for formatting that we mentioned above so that the output behaves in the way that you want. In addition to the four formatting options that are above, you will also be able to control where your output is being sent. Some of the commands that you are able to use in order to control where the output is being sent include:

- Out-Host: this is the command that will be the default so you don't need to make any specifications with this one. It is going to send the output over to the console.

- Out-Default: this is another one that won't need to be specified in the process. it is going to send the output to the default formatting command that is set up. It is also going to delegate this process to the Out-Host.

- Out-File: this is the command that will direct the output to the file that you choose.

- Out-Null: this is the command that is going to delete the output. When you use this, you will see that the PowerShell console isn't going to show any results.

- Out-Printer: this is the command that will direct your output to the printer that you specify.

- Out-String; this is the command that will convert your object into a string array.

Remember that if you need some more help with controlling your output or you want to try out something else with it, you will be able to pull up the Help files to get more assistance with the commands that you want to use.

To use the commands that are listed above, you will need to add them in to the end of the pipeline. A good example of how you can do this in PowerShell includes the following syntax:

Get-Process PS |

Format-List |

Out-File C:\SysInfo\ps.txt

When you use this one, you will see that the output is not going to be displayed on the console of PowerShell. Rather, the system is going to save the contents to the file that you specified in the format (you are able to change it up as you see fit). You do need to make sure that you are sending output files that make sense; sending some text over to a .bmp file would not make that much sense and it would just produce an error without letting you view the output when you try to open the file later on. In addition to letting you direct the output of a file, the Out-File can be useful for allowing you to replace or append content that is already with the current output. If you do not direct it to do otherwise, the PowerShell is going to replace the existing content because this is the default of the program. If you would like to append to the output file, you simply need to add the -append switch to this command so it would look like the following:

Get-Process PS |

Format-List |

Out-File C:\SysInfo\ps.txt

-append

Sorting the Output

In addition to being able to format the output how you would like, there are times when you will want to sort your output as well. To do this, you will want to use the command Sort-Object. This command is going to take the input of the objects of your pipeline and then will sort them based on any criteria that you define. While PowerShell is normally going to stream the results with the help of these pipelines, the Sort-Object command is going to wait until all the results or objects are retrieved before sorting them out. This is basically going to stop the streaming process until all of the sorting is complete. This may not seem like a big deal for smaller returns, but it can slow down the performance when you want to go through large quantities of data.

Even with the idea of this command slowing down the computer a bit, it is still a good command to know how to use. For example, if you would like to get a list of all the items in one folder, you would be able to use the Sort-Object command in order to make this happen. Let's look at an example of how this would work if you would like to get all of the items from the C:\Windows folder to show up on your screen:

dir c:\windows |

where {$_.length -gt 500000} |

sort -property length

-descending

With the code above, the command is going to pass the object from the dir alias on down to the Where-Object, which is shown with the alias of "where". In the Where-Object command we were able to specify (with the help of the -gt part), that we wanted to get the results that were larger than 500,000 bytes. The object will then be sent along this pipeline to the Sort-Object command. When it gets to this part, for which we used sort, it is going to be organized based on the criteria that we specified. In this example, we first sorted the data based on the length with the help of -property length. We were then able to use the -descending switch in order to tell the system that we wanted to have the data show up in descending order. If you didn't put the -descending switch, the system would assume that you wanted it in ascending order and that is how it would show up on the system.

This is a pretty simple formula for getting the information that you want from the system while also going through and sorting it. Of course, you can add in some more properties as you wish, and then the PowerShell system will be able to go through and make the changes that you would like. You can make this as complicated or as simple as you would like based on the information that you want to have show up.

Working with pipelines can make the process a bit easier to work with when it comes to PowerShell. You are not going to be limited on what you are able to have show up on the system and you can send the object through a few different requirements before it comes up on the screen. This can save you a lot of time and as you can see with the examples of this guidebook, it is not too hard for it to all come together and look nice in the system and even as a beginner.

Chapter 4: The Operations and Wildcards of PowerShell

The last chapter spent some time talking about pipelines and how they work to streamline the processes that you want to get done, while also making changes to files and getting the right information sorted out on the screen. You are basically just connecting together a string of commands in order to filter out the objects that you want in the information that appears on the screen.

If you have used some of the other programming languages that are available, you will notice that there are often a lot of operations that are available that will help you to create some expressions inside of your illustrations. This is the same when it comes to using the PowerShell system, you just need to learn how these work within this language as well as which operations you will need to learn in order to get the expressions to work for you. As a review, remember that an expression is basically just a block of code that PowerShell is going to be able to recognize and evaluate, so essentially you are just making blocks of codes that you want to work on this system.

There are many operators that you are able to use which are included in the PowerShell system, and these can often be used within the expressions. Let's take some time in this chapter to look at the different operators and how you can properly use them inside of this system as well as how you can find the properties that come with your different commands.

Operators for Comparisons

The first kind of operators that we are going to use are the comparison operators, and as you can guess, these are the ones that are going to be used in order to compare values. During the times where the comparison is going to be contained inside of the expression, PowerShell is going to compare the values that are to the left and to the right of the operator. There are many comparison operators that you are able to use in your system based on how you would like the system to react. Some of the comparison operators that are popular with PowerShell include:

- -eq: equal to

- -ne: not equal to

- -gt: greater than

- -ge: greater than or equal to

- -lt: less than

- -le: less than or equal to

- -like: uses wildcards in order to find the matching patterns

- -notlik: uses the wildcards in order to find the nonmatching patterns

- -match: uses regular expressions to find matching patterns.

- -notmatch: uses regular expressions in order to find the nonmatching patterns.

- -contains: determines whether the value on the left side of your operator has the same value as the one on the right.

- -notcontains: determines whether the value on the left side of the operator doesn't have the same value as the one on the right.

- -replace: this one will replace part or all of the value that is on the left side of the operator.

You will be able to use any of these operators in order to make a comparison inside of the PowerShell system. If you would like to have the system return all the files in a particular folder that are less than a certain size, you would just need to use the -lt operator, but if you would like to get the files that are larger than a certain size from that file, you would use the -gt operator. You get a lot of freedom in choosing which operator you would like to use just as long as you pick out the right comparison operator that works with what you are looking for in the program.

Wildcards in PowerShell

Another beneficial feature that comes with PowerShell are the wildcards. Let's say that you want to go and search for an item in on of your files, but you don't know the exact name of that file when you are trying to create the new expression that will compare values. What you would be able to do in this situation is to use a wildcard in the operator or the compared values. Some of the wildcards that are supported through the PowerShell system include:

- (*): this is going to match zero or more of any character.

- (?): this one will match any one character that you type out.

- [char-char]: this one is going to match a range of sequential characters

- [char...]: this one is going to match any one character in a set of characters that you define.

The wildcards are going to be used similar to the -like and the -notlike comparison operators to help you to find the files that you are looking for, even if you don't know the complete name or you are confused by which one you want. A good example of how this can all work, including some of the comparison operators as well as the wildcards includes:

et-process |

*where {$_.company -like "*google*"}*

The asterisk is going to be the wildcard that will be used to match zero or more of the characters. This is going to give you some pretty accurate results regardless of whether this name is stored in Windows under some different variations of the name. as long as "google" is somewhere in the name, you are going to get that result to come up on the page.

PowerShell is also able to support what is known as regular expressions. These are going to be based on the classes of regular expressions that are already present in the Microsoft .NET Framework. These are going to be implemented with the help of the -nomatch and -match operators and the support from PowerShell in these expressions is pretty extensive, just like you will find with some of the other .NET languages.

Using Logical Operators

The next type of operators that you are able to use are logical operators. So far, we have just looked at using the operators for when we create a condition and then we want the output, whilst there is only one comparison going on. There will be times when you are using your PowerShell program when you will need to utilize some expressions that will have two or more conditions, such as when multiple comparisons are going to be utilized in order to determine whether the program should take an action or not.

In order to be able to do multiple comparisons while using just one expression, you will need to use a logical operator in the condition, or link it to the condition. The logical operators are going to be used in order to specify what logic can be used when evaluating these multiple conditions. Some of the logical operators that you are able to use inside of the PowerShell program include:

- -and: this is when both conditions will need to be true before the expression is evaluated as true.

- -or: this is when one or both conditions need to be true before the expression is evaluated as true.

- -not: this is when the specified condition needs to be false before the expression is evaluated as true.

- (!): this is when both the conditions need to be false before the expression is evaluated as true.

To get a good understanding of how these logical operators are going to look, let's take some time to go over the following example:

Get-Process |

where {($_.handles -gt 500)

-and ($_.pm -ne 0)}

With this code, we are dealing with two conditions, and both of them are going to be placed into the parentheses. The first one is going to be used to specify that the number of handles has to be bigger than the -gt, which for this formula is going to be 500 for the processes. For the second condition, you will be able to specify that the paged memory, or the pm, size, is not allowed to be equal to 0. Also, using the -and logical operator will allow you to connect both of these conditions inside the expression.

Since these two expressions are connected with the -and operator, they both need to be true for the expression. Only if the file or the document matches up with both of the conditions that you set will it show up in your console. If they only meet one of the conditions and not the other, regardless of which condition they meet, they will not show up on the console. This can help to limit the amount of information that appears when you are performing some of these commands; you can add in as many of the conditions that you need to so that you can just get the information that you want and not all the extras.

Another thing that you are able to use is the -or operator. This one can be placed into the formula like the -and one, but it is going to work differently for what you will be able to get in terms of the results. Let's take a look at what you are going to be able to achieve with this little change.

Get-Process |

where {($_.handles -gt 500)

--or ($_.pm -ne 0)}

Now that you have made a change with the operator that you are using, the system is going to give you a slightly different result than you were getting before. This is the one that you will need to use if you want to get more information, or you would like to get information on more than one condition. For this one, the file that you are searching for can match either the first condition (being greater than 500 for the processes), the second condition (having a paged number that is not 0), or both of them at the same time.

As you can see, you are going to get a lot more information when you are using the -or operator. This will allow you to get all the files and other processes that are able to meet either one of these conditions. It doesn't matter if they get both of the conditions (they are able to get just one), they are going to show up in your console when you use this kind of formula.

Now let's take it a bit further and see what you are able to do when you add together the -not logical operator with the -and operator to show that some specific criteria can't be true when you are looking for something. Here is what the syntax would look like for that:

Get-Process |

where {($_.handles -gt 100)

-and -not($_.company -eq

"Microsoft Corporation")}

With this example, we are telling it that we don't want the handle count to be bigger than 100. We are also specifying that the name of the company you are trying to find can't be Microsoft Corporations. This illustration is going to return all of the processes that are not related to Microsoft for you to look over.

Arithmetic Operators

The next type of operator that you are able to work with when you are inside of PowerShell are arithmetic operators. PowerShell is a coding language that is able to perform mathematical operations. The commands that you will need to use in order to do the mathematical equations will be called arithmetic operators. Some of the arithmetic operators that you may use in PowerShell include:

- (+): this will add two values together

- (-): this one is going to subtract one value from another

- (~): this is going to take a value and convert it into a negative number.

- (*): this one is going to multiply two values together.

- (/): this is going to divide up two values.

- (%): this one is going to return the remainder of numbers that you divided.

So this one is pretty easy to work with. You will be able to use the mathematical operators in order to add things together, to link string values together, and more. They also help out with some of the other commands that you want, such as adding together two different ones that you want to work with. If you would like to find out a bit more about the arithmetic operators and how they may be able to help out with the command that you are trying to write, make sure to look through the help files with the help of the command about_arithmetic_oper.s.

Working with operators can make things a lot easier inside of the PowerShell system. You will find that adding things together, getting the choice of which type of returns you are going to get and more, can make working with PowerShell much easier than before.

Chapter 5: Doing Quotes and Strings in PowerShell

Most of the syntaxes that you will use in PowerShell are going to add in some string values. These are often going to be passed over to the commands in the form of an argument. You will see that the strings will sometimes be enclosed in single quotes and other times they are going to be in a double quote, while occasionally there won't be any quotes around them at all. It is important to know how to handle these strings in the proper way, so let's take a look at the different rules that come along with quoting the strings and how you should do it so that the PowerShell system knows exactly what you are trying to say.

String values

Any time that you put some quotes around text, no matter what kind of text you are writing out, PowerShell is going to handle this like it is a string value. With this in mind, as long as your text doesn't have any special character or any reference scalers, you will be able to choose whether you are going to enclose that text with a double or a single quote. Special characters will need to be treated differently, but we will get to that in a bit.

With regular strings of text, the double and the single quotation marks are going to be the exact same thing. The important part is that the string of text is not going to have any special characters, and that if you start out with a single quote, you will end with the single quote and so on, rather than switching them up part way through. So basically, the following two examples are going to be exactly the same (and produce the same result), even though they are using different quotation marks in them:

Write-Output "String in quotes."

Write-Output 'String in quotes.'

In addition, there are times when you are going to want to use a quote within your string. This is going to work a bit differently than before. You are able to choose to put a single quote within a double quote, or a double quote within a single quote like the following:

Write-Output "String 'in' quotes."

Write-Output 'String "in" quotes.'

If you mix these around and do it the other way, such as having a double inside a double with the quotes, you will find that the system will not read it the same way. Here are two examples of the way that you should avoid when it comes to adding a quote within a quote.

Write-Output "String "in" quotes."

Write-Output 'String 'in' quotes.'

When you type these different variations into the system, you will find that PowerShell is going to interpret them in different ways. For the last two illustrations, you will notice that in the return, the quotes are not going to be displayed and there is a new line that shows up. This is going to happen because PowerShell is going to interpret the one string as multiple strings, which will then result in a line break. PowerShell is going to interpret the word String as the first string, then there will be a line break before the rest is interpreted since it is seen as a new string.

Whenever you are working with quotes, it is important that you aren't messing up the types of quotes. It is a good idea to go through and double check that you aren't missing out on one somewhere in the formula. If you do happen to miss out on a quote, depending on where it is located, you run the possibility of getting trapped inside a loop. With this situation, the loop is going to keep asking you for an entry and no matter what you place inside, you will not be able to pull out of the loop.

If you do happen to miss out on one of the quotes and end up with a loop going on that you can't control, you will just need to go back to the command prompt. You will be able to do this by pressing Ctrl + C to go right back to the beginning and to try it again.

Escaping the special characters

The examples that we have been talking about so far in this book allow you to use either a single quote or a double quote. We have shown how you are able to use both of them, but haven't gone too much into how you can tell the difference between the two and why the computer system is going to see them in different ways. There is a distinction that does exist between them. For example, the single quote is going to handle the string literally while the double quote will allow you to get away from, or escape, the special characters that come up in the text.

When the special character is preceded by the ` or the backtick, it is gong to take on a specific action that would not be accomplishable without these symbols in place. Some of the special characters that you may need to use when you are working in PowerShell include:

- `0: this will insert a value that is null

- `a: this will send an alert (which can be in the sound of a beep or a bell) to the speakers of your computer.

- `b: this one is going to insert a backspace.

- `f: this one is going to insert a form feed.

- `n: this one will insert a new line for you to use with the text.

- `r: this will insert a carriage return.

- `t: this will insert a tab that is going horizontally.

- `v: this is going to insert a tab that is going vertically.

- `': this is going to insert a single quote.

- `": this is going to insert a double quote.

One of the best ways to see how this concept works is to put it into action. The illustration below is going to be one that has had a few characters that have escaped. This is done so that you can see how the text is going to display in your console:

Write-Output ("`n `tText includes: + `

"`n `t" escaped`" characters. `n")

The first character that has escaped in this illustration is the n. you should be able to tell this because it is the first letter in the illustration that is preceded with the help of the backtick. The t is the next one, which is going to result in a tab being inserted into the writing. Notice that the backtick that you are using at the end of your first line will not be used as an escape character, but it is going to be used as a continuation character, showing that the illustration is going to keep on going to the second line. Note also that the n is going to appear two more times in the second line with the t showing up another time. The double quotes will show up around the word "escaped" and they are preceded by the backtick as well so that the double quotes will appear in the output.

Now, if you tried to escape the characters within a string that is enclosed in just a single quote, the special characters, as well as the backticks, will have no results on the output other than the fact that everything is going to be handled literally. So if you went without the double quotes with these special characters, you would get the syntax:

Write-Output '`tindented `n `twords'

When you place this into your console, you are going to just get the same thing back on the console because the single string is going to be taken by its literal meaning. This is something that you will need to remember because in older versions of PowerShell, you were able to write the special characters out with single quotes, but the newer versions have gotten rid of this and if you type in the syntax that we have above, you are not going to get the results that you were looking for.

System.String Object Members

When you are working with strings in PowerShell, it is important to note that all of them are going to be handled like System.String objects. This is going to provide you with a lot of other properties and methods that you can utilize. As mentioned before, the Get-Member command is going to be able to retrieve the members of an object as it is passed down the pipeline. Since the string is also going to be passed along just like the object, you are able to use the Get-Member command for that string as well. A good example of this is the following:

"test output" | Get-Member

By running this, you will see that the string object is able to support several different methods. These can include the Substring and GetType. By scrolling down a bit, you are also going to be able to see the length property, which is going to tell you the number of characters that already exist in that string. So let's pretend that we want to know a bit more about the Substring method that we just mentioned. We would be able to use the Get-Member command in order to retrieve this information with the help of the following illustration:

"test output" |

Get-Member Substring |

Format-List

After you go through and run this illustration, you should be able to observe that there are details that will indicate how to utilize this method in the proper way. There are also two approaches that you are able to use when you are performing this method. They are as follows:

System.String Substring(Int32 startIndex)

System.String Substring(Int32 start Index, Int32 length)

In the first option, you are providing the target string as well an integer. This integer is going to be used in order to specify the position from where you want the substring to start. This is going to cause the substring to have a return that starts in the right position and then will continue on until it reaches the end of the string. This makes it easier if you would like to look at the whole string but want to start from a certain location. So for what we are talking about, if you chose to go with the first option, you could type out something like the following:

("test output").Substring(5).

This will have your test output come up and it will start with a position of 5 on the substring. You can place any number in here that you want to ensure that you are getting the program to start in the location that you require. Make sure that you have the test output in parentheses and that you have a period in place right after the name of the method to keep things easier and working well with PowerShell.

As you saw above, there are two methods that you are able to use so let's take some time to look at the second option. With this one, you are going to provide the target string along with the substrings starting point and the length. So if you would like to start at a specific spot of the string and only want to read a few lines of it (or however much you would like to read through), the second method would be the one you need. The syntax of using this one would look like the following:

("test output).Substring(0,4)

This will allow you to look at the test output starting at the beginning (the 0 is the starting position), and then going out for four characters. Of course you are able to switch out these numbers and get them to behave in the manner that you wish, such as going from the middle of the string to the end, or any other combination.

Working with quotes in PowerShell can make a big difference in the information that is going to come back to you when you place this into the command prompt. Being careful with your quotes and learning how to set some of the parameters that you need can make all the difference in the world as to what will come up on the console.

Chapter 6: Scalers and What They Mean in PowerShell

In this chapter, wee are going to explore the scalers and what they are going to mean when you are working on PowerShell. If you aren't familiar with coding languages and haven't worked with them in the past, scalers may be a foreign word to you, but they are basically a virtual duffel bag that will be used in order to store and then transport data within the PowerShell code. You will find that there are some scalers that are pre-programmed to make things easy for you. You will also see that the scalers are built into the Windows and the PowerShell environment and there is going to be data already allocated to them.

While using the premade scalers can be nice as a beginner and can save you a lot of time and hassle in the long run, there are also going to be times when you will need to create your own scaler. These are going to take on a bit more work and may seem like a challenge to a beginner, but they can be very beneficial.

Since these scalers can be really great for helping you to get things done within the PowerShell environment, it is important to learn a bit more about them, both about the built-in variety as well as the ones that you will have to make on your own.

Built-in Scalers

There are a few different scalers that are already supported within PowerShell. These are going to be able to provide a few types of information, including the PSHOME, $PWD, and more. If you want to see a full list of all the defined scalers for this system as well as the ones that are going to be available inside your current running session, make sure to use the follow illustration to see all the scalers:

dir scaler: | sort name

This illustration is going to start off by using the alias dir. This is going to take the scaler as the argument. This argument is going to refer directly to the scaler drive, which is just one of the drives that is supported by PowerShell. As you should expect, the drive is going to provide access to the scalers as well as their values, including the user defined and the built in scalers.

Once the command succeeds in retrieving the scalers and their values, they will be able to go through your pipeline with the SortObject command. With the illustration above, we used the alias sort to save some space. If you don't want to sort through the information by name, you will see them listed out based on the order they are retrieved rather than in a more organized way.

The list of scalers is going to be really valuable as long as you remember that the list that you are getting may miss out on the $ sign in some cases. To fix this, when you reference the scalers, both the user defined and the built in ones, you will need to have the $ in place in the illustration, otherwise you are going to miss out on some of the scalers that you want to find.

Basically, the dollar sign is used in order to make the scalers easier to find compared to some of the other elements of code. For example, without the dollar sign, it could be hard to determine between the $PWD scaler and the pwd alias that you may be using. When the money sign is in place, you will be able to notice the difference between the two and it is easier to figure out which one you are using.

Any time that you want to get the value of your built in scaler, you will just need to bring up the command script and then enter the name of the scaler that you want to deal with, making sure that you put the dollar sign in front of the name. So when you are ready to pull up the name of the scaler that you want to use, it would look something like this:

$pshome

By running this particular illustration, you are going to get a path to head to the PowerShell home folder. You can do this with any of the built in scalers using the same syntax to make it happen. If at some point you want to get the full list of .dll files that are inside your home folder, just use the following illustration to help you out:

dir $pshome -filter .dll*

There are going to be two types of scalers that are built in and also supported by the PowerShell environment. These are going to be automatic, just like with the $PSHOME that we did above, and preference, which would be like $MaximumErrorCount. The values for the preference scalers can be modified, but you will not be able to make modifications when it comes to the automatic scalers; if you try to make modifications, you will find that you get an error as the return. You can also use the about_preference_scalers to help you to find a full list of the preference scalers and the about_automatic_scaler to help find a list of all the automatic scalers that you are able to use.

Let's take a look at how to use a preference scaler. To modify the value of the preference scaler, you will just need to use the assignment operator in order to adjust the value. The assignment operator that you will want to use is (=_. The preference scaler $MaxiumuErrorCount, for example, is going to be used in order to specify the depth of the error history log in your current session. If you change or update the value, it is going to persist until you either make another change or you end the session you are currently in.

Any time that you want to make a change with this particular formula, you would just need to write out the formula to do so, making sure that you use the equal sign (=) in order to set it up. Let's say that you want to increase the value of the scaler from 200 to 250. You would simply need to write out the illustration to look like the following to make this happen:

$maximumerrorcount = 250.

You can make this number change to anything that you would like, but you get the idea that as long as it is a preference scaler, you will be able to make the adjustments and see what can happen. Remember that if you are working with the automatic scalers, you will not be able to make changes at all and if you try, you will find that it is going to result in an error response.

Scalers: Environment

At times, you may want to get a hold of the scalers that are present in the Windows environment. This is something that you are able to do when you use the Env drive within PowerShell. If you would like to get a full list of the Windows environment scalers along with their values, you will be able to use the following illustration in order to look at the list and sort them out based on their names:

dir env: | sort name

Similar to the built in scalers and the user defined scalers, the list of environment scalers is not going to include the prefix that will be needed for them to be included within the PowerShell code when you are referencing them. However, you need to remember that there is a difference in the prefixes that are used with environment scalers, as compared to the other scalers we have discussed.

In the user defined scalers and the built in scaler, you will remember that we used the $ as the prefix. But when using the environmental scalers, we will have to use the $env at the beginning of the name of these scalers any time that we are going to reference them. For example, any time that we want to find out the value of the windir environment scaler, we would need to use the following illustration:

#env:windir

If you would like to get the full list of all the .dll files that are located inside the home folder on Windows, you would use the following illustration:

dir $env:windir -filter .dll*

Another thing that you should know is that you are able to change up the values of the environment scalers that you are using. For example, let's say that you want to make some modifications of the value of the HOMEPATH from \Documents and Settings\administrator and change it over to be \Documents and Settings\administrator\home. To get this done, you would just need to use the (+) operator and then add in the \home string to the value of HOMEPATH. To do this, use the following illustration to get it done:

$env:homepath =

$env:homepath + "\home"

Just like with the scaler that we mentioned in the past section, this new change is going to keep on working until you either make another change (or change it back), or until you end your current session.

List Defined Scalers

In some of the scripting languages that you want to use, you will need to explicitly state out the scaler before you use it. PowerShell makes this a bit easier because it won't restrict you and make you go through all that effort. You will just need to assign the value to the scaler and then you are set to go. For example, you will be able to use the following illustration in order to assign the string one-two to the scaler $var1:

$var1 = "one two"

By defining the scaler in this way, you are basically using the New-scaler command. This is going to end up providing two arguments, which will be the name of the scaler as well as the value. If you do use the New-scaler command option, as well as the Removescaler, Set-scaler, or Clear-scaler command, you will not need to use the $ sign in front of the name of the scaler.

In most cases, you will want to stick with the first example of what we posted here to keep things simple.

Other Data Types

In this section we are going to spend some time looking at the other things that you will need to keep in mind when it comes to setting up a user defined scaler. To get started, you will first

35

need to create the $var1. You can do so with the following illustration:

$var1 = "one two"

You can also get the value from just typing in $var1, but we are assigning a new string to the variable, the "one two" and it is going to be stored as the string object. Remember that you can always verify an object type by using the GetType() method using the illustration using $var1.gettype().

It is also good to remember that when you are creating a new scaler, you are not going to be limited to just going with the string values. For example, you will be able to assign an integer to the scaler value with the following illustration:

$var1 = 123; $var1.gettype()

By running the illustration above, the PowerShell will automatically store the value and do so using the correct type, which in this case is going to be Int32. After running this illustration, you are going to see that there are multiple illustrations that are returned. If you would like to manually terminate the illustration, then you should just add in a semicolon. The semicolon can help you to run more than one illustration in one line, as long as you are using the semicolon to separate them out.

You can also take the time to assign values other than integers or strings when you are creating a new scaler. The process is going to be pretty much the same and you will use the following illustration:

$var1 = 12.34; $var1.gettype()

$var1 = get-date; $var1.gettype()

The first illustration is going to be used in order to store the value type under Double while the second illustration above is going to be used by PowerShell in order to store the value type as GetDate.

Now, there are times when you are going to want to append the text that is already part of a string value within the scaler. You will be able to follow the same approach that you did for adding in the text. The illustration that you would use in order to append the string of text that is already in place will include the following:

$var1 = "one two three"; $var1

$var1 = $var 1 + "four"; $var1

As you can see, you took the first string that was "one two three" and then in the second line you went in and added in the string of "four". You should end up with a new string in your scaler that is going to say "one two three four". You can add in anything that you would like to this part, perhaps going up to ten for example.

These are just a few of the things that you are able to do with the scalers that you are working with. You can also use them to make references in your commands or you can use them to make some of your own arguments.

Chapter 7: The Drives and Providers

When you are working with PowerShell, you are able to use different folders and files, but first you will need to provide the right path name. The pathname is always going to begin with C:\ followed by the rest of the name that comes with the folder or file that you want. Whenever you want to access a specific file system resource, you must make sure that you are providing PowerShell with the correct name of the drive or you will need to have the drive implied inside of the command's context. For instance, if you want to have a list of information returned from your current workstation, you do not need to list out the specific drive.

There are also drives outside of the file system drives that are going to be supported by PowerShell, and these are going to give you a lot of access to the different data stores that you need to do some amazing things inside of this program. One example is the scaler drive that you worked on before. This drive is going to help you to access all of the built in scalers that are available with PowerShell. We also took a little look at the Env drive that can help you to get access to the environment scalers.

In this chapter, we are going to talk a bit more about some of the other drives that you are able to use, as well as how you are able to utilize them with the help of PowerShell. We will take a look at some of the drives that are built into the system as well as how to create whole new drives when you want. With the help of the information in this chapter, you will be able to create drives, access the certificate store, the registry, files system, and some of the other data stores as you need them.

PowerShell Providers

The first thing that you need to understand is that the core that you need from data stores will reside inside the PowerShell provider. One of the providers with this system is the Microsoft .NET. this layer is going to show up between the PowerShell and the data and it is going to allow you to connect to the data stores with various mechanisms in the service. For example, you will be able to use the Get-Children command to access the file system, certificate data stores, and registry.

There are a lot of different providers that are built into the PowerShell. To view a full list of all the providers that can use with this environment, you would just need to write out Get-PSProvider | select Name. there is a lot of potential for a variety of providers to become available to use. This is because you are able to extend out the PowerShell system. You can locate these providers, even if they aren't already on PowerShell, in order to use them in the way that you see fit. These ones will no longer be called PowerShell Providers; rather, they are going to be known as customer providers.

If you are interested in seeing a list of all the built in providers that come with the PowerShell system, look at the list below:

- Alias: this is the aliases that you are able to call the various commands that you want to use inside of PowerShell.

- Certificate: this is a process through Windows that is for digital signature certificates.

- Environment: this is a Windows environment scaler

- FileSystem: this is the Windows file system drives, files, and folders.

- Function: this is the PowerShell functions.

- Registry: this is the Windows registry.

- Scaler: these are all the PowerShell scalers that we talked about earlier in this guidebook.

As you can see, some of these processes are available through the Windows programming. The providers above are gong to be a big part of the coding process, but you will barely be able to see them within the PowerShell. You are most likely going to see all the different drives inside of the system that are used to access the providers rather than seeing the providers themselves.

The built in drives

So first, we are going to take a look at some of the PowerShell drives that are already inside the system and move on from there. The PowerShell drives are often utilized in order to return data from the providers. For example, the file system data from the file system provider is going to be exposed by the PowerShell drives that already correspond with the system's Windows drives. The C drive is going to access the data by the file system provider for example, which will basically expose the Windows C drive in the system. If you would like to see a list of the PowerShell drives as well as their providers, use the following illustration:

Get-PSDrive | sort Provider, Name

With the help of this illustration, you are going to sort by the provider first before receiving the name. this is going to result in all the providers being grouped together, and then you can see how many of the drives are supported by each of the providers. This illustration can also be used in order to display some of the root information that you need so you can use it to locate the target data store.

If you would like to get some more information on some of the specific drives, you will just need to use the Get-PSDrive command followed by the information that you would like to receive. For example, if you would like to format a list, you would just need to type out Get-PSDrive Function | Format-List to get this done.

Create a new drive

While there are a lot of great drives that you are able to use that are already built into the PowerShell system, there are times when you will want to create a new drive on this system. These are going to be based on some of the providers that are already existing, which is going to make it easier to make the commands and illustrations, but when you use this information, you will be able to create something new that works the way that you want.

Let's try making a new drive for PowerShell. First you are going to need to use the New-PSDrive command like you did before. Let's take a look at an example of a syntax that we would use while working on the drive named ps.

New-PSDrive -Name ps

-PSProvider FileSystem -Root $pshome

This illustration is first going to identify the name of the new drive, and then it will go on to name the provider, and then the root. When you are running this illustration, the PowerShell is going to create the drive and then will display the information that you need about the drive. You will notice that any information that is displayed is actually going to be the root name, rather than the scaler name. Once this new drive has been created, you will then be able to use it in the same way that you would with the built in drives. If you would like to change the locale for operating to the newly created drive, you just need to use the following illustration:

*cd ps: *

There are also times when you will need to remove or delete a drive that you created or defined, and you will simply need to use the Remove-PSDrive command to do so. It is important to keep track of the drives that you are in because you are not going to be able to delete a drive that you are working in. So once you change the operating locale, you will be able to use the following illustration in order to remove that drive;

cd C: \; Remove-PSDrive ps.

One other thing to remember about these drives is that they are only going to persist in the session that they are created. This can be helpful because you are not going to have to go through and delete or remove the processes or the drives unless there is a specific reason for doing so. They will automatically delete once you exit out of the system.

Creating drives can help to determine where you are going to be working inside the system. While you can choose to work with the built in ones, you can also design some of your own based on what you would like to do with the system.

Conclusion

Thanks again for taking the time to read this book!

You should now have a good understanding of how to use Powershell!

If you enjoyed this book, please take the time to leave me a review on Amazon. I appreciate your honest feedback, and it really helps me to continue producing high quality books.

www.ingramcontent.com/pod-product-compliance
Lightning Source LLC
LaVergne TN
LVHW050148060326
832904LV00003B/61